If Not These Things

If Not These Things

Poems by

Kenneth Chamlee

© 2022 Kenneth Chamlee. All rights reserved.
This material may not be reproduced in any form, published,
reprinted, recorded, performed, broadcast,
rewritten or redistributed without
the explicit permission of Kenneth Chamlee.
All such actions are strictly prohibited by law.

Cover design by Shay Culligan
Cover image by jplenio from Pixabay
Author image by Juls Buckman

ISBN: 978-1-63980-158-9

Kelsay Books
502 South 1040 East, A-119
American Fork, Utah 84003
Kelsaybooks.com

For Teresa, who believes

Also by Kenneth Chamlee

Absolute Faith
Logic of the Lost
The Best Material for the Artist in the World

Acknowledgments

Sincere appreciation is made to the following publications in which these poems first appeared, some in slightly different versions or with different titles:

Ariel VII: "Diminuendo"
Asheville Poetry Review: "Accident" (now "Just Past Enon Baptist Church"), "Fallout Shelter, 1961" (now "Our Neighbor Builds a Fallout Shelter, 1961"), and "The Mockingbird at the Writers' Conference"
Blue Mountain Review: "One Day" (now "If Not These Things")
Blue Pitcher: "In My Next Life" (now "Planning My Next Incarnation")
ByLine Magazine: "In Concert"
Canary: "Day Tour"
A Carolina Literary Companion: "Flying at Night" (now "The New Constellations")
Charlotte Poetry Review: "The Slipping"
Chiaroscuro: "Fantasia Afterthought," and "Real World" (now "Freshmen Being Told About the Real World"
Cold Mountain Review: "Gray" (now "Before the Fog Burns Off")
College English: "Housefire" (now "After the Doctor Said No")
Coraddi: "The Wilderness Experience"
Crucible: "Renaissance"
Cumberland Poetry Review: "The English Professor's Flag Football Game" and "The Pull"
Diagram: "Changing Wallets" (now "Shifting Pictures")
The Greensboro Review: "That Long Delayed But Always Expected Something That We Live For"
GSU Review: "Oh! Blessed Rage For Order"
Kakalak: "After the Adventure Films," "Ceiling Fan" (now "Before I Even Get Out of Bed"), "Kitchen Inventory," "Match Play" (now "Match Play With Mr. D"), "The Moon's Face Opens in Song," "Seed," and "Zodiac" (now "Embracing My Sign at the Chinese Restaurant")

The Lyricist: "35,000 Feet" (now "Graphing the Landscape at 30,00 Feet"), and "Warrant" (now "Playing Death")
Main Street Rag: "Confusion" (now "State of Confusion"), "Goldfish Diary" (now "Goldfish with Issues"), and "Street Preacher" (now "A Lesson on the Immaterial")
Montana Mouthful: "The Jigsaw Puzzle from the Second-Home Thrift Store"
Pinesong: "Iconography" (now "Rural Icon"), "New Song," "Please Stand," "Ritual," and "What the Famous Writer Said"
Pisgah Review: "A Face to Meet the Faces," "The First Ten Minutes of the Local News," and "Weather Map"
Runes–Signals: "Sign People"
Tar River Poetry: "Counting My Daughter's Boyfriends on One Hand"
Teach/Write: "The Fossil Poem"
Word Journal: "After Deciding to Divorce" and "Pulse"

"Absolute Faith" appeared in the *Chester H. Jones National Poetry Competition Winners 1999,* and was selected for the Poetry in Plain Sight initiative (NC Poetry Society), 2021. "Before the Fog Burns Off" (as "Gray") was reprinted in *Cold Mountain Review, Special 35th Anniversary Issue*. "Friends in Denali" was printed in *The Cataloochee Bridge* (Old Mountain Press). "The Mockingbird at the Writers' Conference" was reprinted in *Webster's Reading Room* (Old Mountain Press). "Playing Death" was reprinted in *Old Tales* (Old Mountain Press). "The Slipping" was reprinted in *Lights in the Mountains* (Winding Path Publishing).

These poems first appeared in the chapbook *Absolute Faith* (ByLine Press): "Crawl Space" (now "Right Now in the Attic Crawl Space"), "The Logic of Dreams," "Magic" (now "Resolve"), "Midnight Crossing," "The Void," "Walking Home Past Sprinklers," "Warning," and "Words" (now "Another Word").

These poems first appeared in the chapbook *Logic of the Lost* (Longleaf Press): "Bringing a Poem to the Teacher" and "The Magician on the First Day of School."

"After Deciding to Divorce" was the winner of the *Word Journal* Poetry Prize, 2003. "Oh! Blessed Rage For Order" was the winner of the *GSU Review* Writing Award in 1999.

****

Many thanks to Keith Flynn and Margaret Brown for suggestions on early versions of this manuscript. For helpful comments on recent poems, I am grateful to Jane Curran, Anne Green, Lottie Erickson, Greg Lobas, and Kathleen Calby. I am happily indebted to Tonya Staufer for her laughter and encouragement, and most especially to the sharp eyes and ears of Karen Luke Jackson whose keen sensibilities made this a better book.

Contents

I

Weather Map	21
The Wilderness Experience	22
Walking Home Past Sprinklers	24
The Logic of Dreams	25
Dark Edge	26
State of Confusion	27
Freshmen Being Told About the Real World	28
Bringing a Poem to the Teacher	30
The Fossil Poem	31
The New Constellations	32
Playing Death	33
Our Neighbor Builds a Fallout Shelter, 1961	34
Graphing the Landscape at 30,000 Feet	36
Match Play with Mr. D	37
Dirt Devil	38
The Magician on the First Day of School	39
Another Word	41
'That Long Delayed But Always Expected Something That We Live For'	42
After the Adventure Films	43
The Mockingbird at the Writers' Conference	44

II

Seed	47
Pulse	48
Just Past Enon Baptist Church	49
The Void	50
The First Ten Minutes of the Local News	51
What Falls Out	52

Warning	53
The Slipping	54
Ritual	55
Before I Even Get Out of Bed	56
After Deciding to Divorce	57
Embracing My Sign at the Chinese Restaurant	58
Planning My Next Incarnation	59
Fantasia Afterthought	60
Shifting Pictures	62
'A Face To Meet The Faces'	63
Renaissance	64
The English Professor's Flag Football Game	65
Swing Away	67
Gong Show	68
Rural Icon	69
The Jigsaw Puzzle from the Second-Home Thrift Store	70

III

A Lesson on the Immaterial	73
Sign People	74
What the Famous Writer Said	75
Friends in Denali	76
After the Doctor Said No	77
Right Now in the Attic Crawl Space	78
Midnight Crossing	79
Diminuendo	80
Counting My Daughter's Boyfriends on One Hand	81
Kitchen Inventory	83
Goldfish with Issues	85

In Concert	86
Resolve	87
The Moon's Face Opens in Song	88
Day Tour	89
The Pull	90
'Oh! Blessed Rage For Order'	92
Before the Fog Burns Off	94
Please Stand	95
Absolute Faith	96
If Not These Things	97
New Song	98

For poems are not words, after all, but fires for the cold, ropes let down to the lost…
—Mary Oliver

I

Weather Map

The jet stream dipped down like a gourd,
ladling away summer, putting out fireflies
and spilling the language of barriers:
trough, ridge, pressure.

Though it makes no sense to say
the weather is wrong or
out of sorts, we insist on tying
common rags to the tail of its numinous kite:
outburst, rage, calm.
A high cloud like a cold morning word,
followed by an arid week of silence.

Still, the weather feels strange today,
sleet ticking my nylon jacket as I
range the same miles of field and woods
I do almost every day, no matter.
Seventy degrees yesterday, and a sky as blank

as the green screen behind a weatherman,
figures ghosted on a small monitor,
every forecast an illusion.

The Wilderness Experience

for David

Somewhere below the balsam summit,
the trail we followed from the valley
is gone. Wide as a boulevard
beside our morning camp, it narrowed
away from the river, collapsed to a suggestion
of ferns, and now has disappeared
beneath stump-spill and jackstraw trees.
The last blaze mark was an hour ago,
and cryptic light is slanting across
our unshouldered packs. We are lost.

When the Puritans sagged to that rocky coast,
they did not know the sea of trees
before them was as vast as the ocean behind;
they knew only their fears: beasts
and devils, unimaginable darkness.
They hacked graveyards and clearings,
roughed out scaffolds and cabins,
each acre of ragged stumps a sanctuary.

In the deep gloom of rhododendron,
I recall how every season someone
strays from a mountain trail and dies,
someone who did not expect to, and I
begin to understand the Puritans.
I see myself in stiff clothes,
swinging an axe against the wall
of woods around me, wanting it gone,
wanting to be back at the river
by a dwindling fire, not pulling myself
through heath-hells and gullies choked with roots.

With the logic of the lost, we grope
the way we came, the hardest way,
toward what we think we know.

Walking Home Past Sprinklers

Six whales surface in the grass
between two buildings. All at once
they spout the sweat of caves,
plumes of thermal steam.

How did they come to be here?
Did they dive through oceans of granite,
cruise beneath mountain snowpelts
straining magma through pale baleen?

Trees on the lawn drift upright
like verdant buoys. Perhaps it's not whales
out of place here. I watch from the walk
as they dive down, equivocal, together.

The Logic of Dreams

Reporters surround my bed, elbowing,
shoving bouquets of cameras
at my stubbled face, quizzing me
on how it feels and when did I know,
zooming in on my skewed pajamas
and electrokinetic hair.

Inside the rented cabin
the California blonde steps
into the shower with me. Her tan
melts and her hair streaks gray.
A nipple washes off,
the small pink cup of it
covers the drain, colors pooling.
I panic and lunge dripping
into a mirrored lobby.

At eight in the morning my students
yawn and flip lamely through their books.
I haven't shown up again.
And now the truth I cannot prompt—
am I gauzed in dream or failure,
webbed to the night's edge
with my face in my hands?

Dark Edge

Why not, I thought, the wind being calm and the afternoon
pale as my son's hair, so I said *Yes, you can go*
with the men of Lake Jeanette Fishing Club
who give two-dollar rides on a Sunday afternoon,
swinging orange-vested toddlers into johnboats
and electric-motored canoes.

The boats scattered into zigzags, beelines and curves,
each captain styling the trip to his craft, and off went my son
zippered into a high-visibility preserver hugging his coil of ribs.
I was thinking I hadn't asked the skipper's name or even
gotten a good look at his face under that tugged-down ball cap
as the boat puttered into a far cove and disappeared.

How long is long enough? One minute? Three minutes? Five?
On the dock of a small lake not four miles from our house
I listened to a toolbox of dads saw up yesterday's scores
    and believed
the planks were buckling under me like untendoned bones.
Most thoughts slip like leaves down a spillway but some
catch a dark edge and eddy forever.
                           When the boat reappeared
my son waved like a flame in a signal torch.
As I grabbed him off the dock he pitched back,
stiff-arming us into a capital Y, shrilling *Guess what we saw?!*
I touched his chattering mouth, watched the boatman lift
another child, and thought, it's all right, nothing happened, and
what, what was I thinking?

State of Confusion

Confusion should be straightforward, like this:
you're on page twelve of a thick Victorian novel
and the sixty-fourth character has just been introduced—
a cousin's maid, Elizabeth, whom they call Lillibet,
or you might be taking a test in a high-ceilinged room
with tall, unshaded windows and the formulas
you memorized have burned off like mist,
or you've stalled in the dairy aisle studying
calories, fat grams, calories *from* fat and why
does it matter what you eat? You die anyway.

If confusion is a state, then today you are its capital,
a dim city with traffic lights holding yellow,
restaurants with no menus and reticent waiters,
a city of unnumbered elevator buttons, signless
malls, marquees without titles or times
and newspapers that never use names.

Freshmen Being Told About the Real World

Your parents' admonition hangs like a dialogue balloon
before they wave and drive away. Now you know
what to get ready for, what
you'd better-not-waste-this-chance to earn.

And you try to picture it, the real world,
that glittering city with its tangible buildings,
concrete problems, stoic citizens
manifest with purpose, where time is measured
nine-to-five, fifty weeks a year for thirty years,
not 10 to 10:50, MWF, for a semester.

And how daunting that future world must seem
as you have merely moved into a one-room
arrangement with a stranger in an unexplored town
and swapped your familiar hand of friends
for several decks of blank face cards.
When classes start you must oblige
multiple bosses whose demands are
a penumbra of portent, two words that leap
from the SAT Essay and whose meanings
you may unpack later.

Since arriving you have answered the question
"Where you from?" so many times you
no longer believe you are from there, it
doesn't exist, the green interstate signs removed
and the exit ramp a receding arc of white flowers
planted by the D.O.T., a small brass marker
with the dates of your town, your former life.

Cast ashore on this island of friendly natives
you are welcomed with feasts and placement tests,
bonfires and lectures on tropical responsibility.

Urged toward an amphitheater for skits about rum
and recycling, you imagine this island's highest crag,
whips of mist trailing like a trimmed sail, and you can
slip away and climb, pull your way past dark roots
and dripping moss, past rare orchids pale as morning
till you stand looking down at the canopy
vibrant with birdsong and innumerable hues of green,
down at the white page of beach, each wave
adding its salt and story to the strand.

Bringing a Poem to the Teacher

Office hours are over, but I wave her in.
She slips me her poem on a clipboard,
like a chart, and waits, clicking her nails
along the curved arm of my rocker.
As she moves her rings from finger
to finger, I lift the scripted sheet
and find her more naked than knowing.

Look at this girl: her face is bright
as a scalpel. She is tan and thin,
but her poem is fat and old, and under
its pale skin swells a common revelation—
lost innocence, rejection, and despair.
I am new at this and eager to believe
the truth is what she wants
so I lift it out and hold it to her, benign.

Immediately I know I have blundered:
her face drains to gray. "Of course,
I'm only guessing," I say, sponging
equivocations, but she lifts her cobalt eyes
and sees that I am lying.
                         So we sit,
silent as scrubbed tile, aware of both
our failures. And I wonder, can she accept
this bungled examination and try again?
Or will she keep herself as close
as the blanched page in her hand,
adding poetry to her list of heart's betrayals.

The Fossil Poem

Can any poem endure
like an ambered ant's
clear vesture?

Can any green thoughts insist
like riverbed ferns
eons pressed?

Ideas are as fragile
as atmospheres, breathe
mineral

words, burn carbon's heat
with each start.

The New Constellations

Blue points of light suggest
a Milky Way below: the faint
prick and surge of headlights,
quasar towers, a nebula of mall.

A quick throttle-back, a second
of weightless coasting; the head's gyro
corrects the winglight's dip,
argues direction out of darkness.

Details effaced, memory configures
a slash of freeway, a grand opening's
searchlight taper. Imperceptibly,
this lower galaxy thins to patternless glints.

The new constellations emerge:
Amanita, Enterprise.
All we are flies with us.

Playing Death

When blackbirds cherry-drunk in spring
splattered our drying wash, we played out
in the backyard and died. The purplish
berries were no good for eating, unlike
the red eye-bites our parents speared in drinks,
so we slapped handfuls of gore to T-shirts,
fought in storied battles—twin pines were

Samson's pillars, the dog Delilah;
we were dropped in the cold sand at Normandy,
hacked by Roman swords forged from stilts
then clocked by a black knight's tetherball mace.
We toppled off stepladder cliffs into grass seas,
fell to muskets, revolvers, submachine brooms,
Apache lances and arcs of longbow arrows.

Our death throes were precise and graceful:
overlapped hands to the heart, spine arched,
knees sagging in a spiral collapse,
a yodeled scream, the grimace without pain.
We lingered in eloquence, brave farewells
and tributes, wild grief for fallen comrades.
Smiles flicked across the masks of our repose—
we bounced up, scrambling to the jet-swings
bloodless and bloody, lifting away from scuffed earth.

Our Neighbor Builds a Fallout Shelter, 1961

When the bulldozer gouged a crater in his yard,
we prayed he was building a pool. But a crane
swung a bus-sized drum over his house, easing it
down to workmen who leveled and braced it.

At night a bluish ray dazzled
the silver underleaves of his maples,
flaring out like a hole to the earth's center
as he sang above his clatter and drill-whine.

For another week we gaped at him
grappling with roped whiskey boxes,
shoving them through the tight hatch
that sprouted in his backyard like a mushroom.

One evening, over the fence, he offered us a tour.
The earth above was red and mounded
and at the bottom of the ladder looking
past my hands at an eight-by-ten of sky,

I remembered them locked behind my head
as I squatted in a windowless
corridor at school, cringing
beneath an endless, strident bell.

A power cord snaked from his basement. "Of course,
we'll use flashlights and candles, later on."
"What about smoke?" I asked, and he let me wring
the ventilation crank. Bunks hinged to the curved walls

were leveled with chains. Shelves of canned peaches,
tuna and beans. Boxes of rice
and instant potatoes. Jugs of water.
Two decks of cards and a stack of *Outdoor Life*.

For days after I sketched subs and bathyscaphes,
trying to pencil away the test-specter
of Nevada desert lifting in a white bubble
that rippled the fusing sand, but every week

our neighbor bragged loudly to someone new
about how he could have had a mountain cabin
or a piece of chigger-infested lake frontage,
but, no, he was smarter than that.

Graphing the Landscape at 30,000 Feet

The glint of diminishing cars
refutes motionless ground. Roads
lace out like veins, flowing
around mercurial lakes, school buses
parked like kernels of yellow corn,
the ribbed fan of a drive-in theater.

Fences and hedgerows fade
into the blue inlaid stamp
of swimming pools. Oil tanks
cluster like a button card,
flat mountains routed
for high-tension wires.

The hyperbolic curve of cooling towers
shapes a sense of boundary.
New wheat lines up against fallow.

Match Play with Mr. D

Morning blisters at Lombrices Resort
and Death has an early tee time. He was up
at first blaze, sharpening finger-bones
into slender neck-like tees
to prop the skullish balls before
each hole's annunciatory whack.
He has put on red shoes with spikes,
black spats and argyle knickers,
a pinked-out plaid shirt and tartan tam.
Death has no taste, of course; he wears it all.

He slashes his way around the course, slicing his drives,
bashing worm-burners that furrow the fairways.
He blasts out of buried lies and hacks through wiregrass rough,
swinging his nine iron like a scythe.
On every hole he lags up then
misses a putt shorter than an emphysemic breath.

At last he reaches the eighteenth green, yanking the flag
like a grenade's pin. His playing partner
hasn't fared much better, but they are even,
both putting for bogey. The man is nervous and
afraid to win, so he shanks the putt and shrugs.
Death takes a last read, one final drag
on his cigarette, and wins by a stroke.
"Actually, I prefer to play in the afternoon," he says,
"Especially when I am on holiday."

Dirt Devil

The upright vacuum won't suck a single string
stranded on the bedroom carpet. I've pushed it
back and forth a half-dozen times, but the string
just flips into a new loop like
a snake on a busy highway.

I toe the power, drop the tall faceplate
and find the yellow sack packed
as tight as a bag of bread flour. I unwedge it
from its cardboard port and carry it,
carefully as a baby, through the house
to the outside can. I hold it away, lifted
like a little god, its round rubbery mouth
still seeking the hard blue breast of the Dustmother.

I replace the paper lung, breathe easier,
and to the drone of a thousand wings
I dance with the devil in the corners of my home.

The Magician on the First Day of School

August. Puddles in the flooded meadow
mirror the yielding sky. My son and I
are wrapped in silent thought. In the dark curve
before the river and the open road,
a farm is disappearing behind nettles
and bracken gone to seed: a crosscut saw
nailed to a flaking barn, brown rabbits
in a rotted hutch.
                    "Dad, will I learn
magic at school? Or just the stuff I need?"
As if magic weren't. I ask him why.
"If I were magic, I'd make the river go over
the bridge."
             "Like the flood?"
                               "No, I want it
to jump over like a rainbow. But when
I say 'abracadabra,' nothing happens."

Already, words have failed him. He thinks power
is in the utterance and the waving of hands.
And why not? For six-and-a-half years one word
would get him juice, tied shoes, eager parents
game-splayed and smiling on the toy-strewn carpet.
Now, with the alphabet under his ingenuous cape,
why shouldn't he expect the unexpected?
How many cartoon chases seen that ended
in smashed, pan-shaped faces shaken off?
How many hounded ducks who sprinted up
floating ropes, and then beyond the ropes,
hauling themselves frantically through braided air?

My son is walking towards his lucky teacher
now, still holding my hand, but he lets go
and runs and shouts goodbye and this is not
the beginning I imagined, not the ending.
His unpracticed leaving makes me think
that desire and the right words might
be enough to lift that choking river
and snap it toward the iridescent sky.

Another Word

Odd, isn't it,
how the lay of words is sometimes
poetry, sometimes
an insurance policy or other ruck.

How the same words, more
or less, explode
one time, freeze another;
how we always know

one word late
what is one word too many,
but never know the one word
that will speak perfection.

How there are removes of love
the word cannot reach, the way
the same beach can be a mist of silver,
a dependable tide, a fog

heavy as a secret, a single drift-tree
twisted deep in the sand,
its branches gray as marble
and as cold.

How to you words are impulse
and momentum, a river rippling
around the snags, and to me
words must be measured and cut,

laid as tight as deck planking
so they will not leak; how we can even
talk—another word
as illusive as love.

'That Long Delayed But Always Expected Something That We Live For'

The Glass Menagerie

For a hopeful friend,
a gentleman caller himself:
some handsome architect with a red Porsche—
one not enamored with his analyst
nor suing his ex for custody—
someone she could wait to go to bed with.

For a colleague at the office,
a Bayliner with flybridge and stereo,
a cruise down the Intracoastal
and on over to Great Harbour Cay,
lounging beneath intimate Bahamian sunsets,
maybe lime daiquiris for breakfast.

For me, it's the rail trip from Skagway
to Whitehorse, a cabin in Denali Park,
shooting *Geographic* slides of humpbacks
sounding in the straits, icebergs
calved in Glacier Bay, stunning me
with a crush of joy.

After the Adventure Films

So many ways to fall.
A roped climber swings his curved axe
and the ice wall cracks, drops like a stiff veil.
A kayaker in slow-blue-motion arcs
toward the plunge basin of a hundred-foot falls.

In the fogged camp of my car that first
catch-breath moment lets go an avalanche
of kisses, a white rush beyond gravity
and physics as we unclip like reckless climbers,
free but not solo, and no looking down.

The Mockingbird at the Writers' Conference

The plagiarist solos every morning at sunrise,
and loudly. We hear him high on the cornice,
gray throat working a line
clear and extravagant, urging us
out of our spare and stifling rooms.

From the vast water oak by the library
he recites before the morning lecture—
a sonnet of tanager, thrush couplet,
the caustic free verse of squirrels.
We hate him for his casual mastery

of form, and for being
the spontaneous poet we all want to be—
each borrowed phrase raised and melded
into art, each silvery intonation
the music and the mirror of deceit.

II

Seed

I hung a red birdfeeder under the carport eave,
replacing an unwatered fern. No birds came.
After I swept away the brown curls and scattered
a coaxing trail, three doves ruffled out of the mist
to bob and peck. Wrens built a nest under my
bicycle seat, but nothing drew to the feeder.
Even the squirrels ignored it, their bodies and tails
scribing cursive m's as they looped around the yard.

This morning as the coffeemaker gurgled and hissed,
a hummingbird zipped to the feeder, paused,
whirred a quick circuit, vanished, returned,
touched the tray with its needle beak before I
blinked it away.

How many times have I tossed chaff
instead of seed, poured seed
instead of nectar?

I stared into the waking yard
long enough to watch shadows
disown the stacked flowerpots
and inch away.

Pulse

A traffic signal pulses red and green together—
mechanical glitch, the yellow trucks soon
with wooden ladders and two wheels on the curb.

Stopgo stayleave   what clear ambivalence
keepgive hidetrust   not dilemma,
those ragged choices of midnight
sweat and prayer, but importunate law:
the hand giving the hand
taking away.

Edge toward the intersection,
claim the green but not wholly—
foot poised above brake,
fist over horn.

Just Past Enon Baptist Church

My stomach flips. I know
that car. And there is the beard
and belly of my friend he is
standing thank God talking.

I pull over, return his nod.
Glass flakes wink from his shirt.
Called from work, his wife floats,
hand on her mouth, staring
at their absurd wagon, passenger side
chevroned to the gear shift.

I take her arm. Blue strobes
lash our silence over and over.
Winches, brooms, signatures,
and still her hand at her mouth.

The Void

"A body found in a car that was discovered submerged in a pond may be that of a woman who has been missing for twelve years, authorities said today."
—The Asheville Citizen-Times, April 16, 1992

She wiped cereal from the baby's chin
and kissed her. Told her parents not to wait
up. She'd stop and get the milk and Winstons,
and Friday begin looking for her own place.

How that seared family must have mourned
and hated her. Their irresolute hearts, flaring
each hour with gossip and nightmare, burned
finally to impalpable ash, as honestly as dropping

an earring, or glancing at a frayed sleeve.
Three seconds of jolting bumps, a splash,
and then the black moment of weightless disbelief,
before the screams, the rush, the startled fish.

The First Ten Minutes of the Local News

A bridge collapses beneath your car
but our coiffed hair and capped teeth
assuage the Omega Chi who rushed
back to his burning fraternity house to save
an elderly couple knocked from their shoes by
Christmas presents which tumbled when the first shots were
brought to you by Nasanall which offers relief from
standing in an aluminum johnboat where Smith
saw the clouds flashing but couldn't get
any cleaner than this just look at the shine on that
charred stereo, fused tackle box, white
Taurus fenders rended with a Sawzall
and dropped into the landfill of your living room
where we'll be right back.

What Falls Out

Hustling along a sidewalk, running late but
Wow! like I stepped barefoot on a treble hook,
so I stop, wag my shoe, walk on, but something
digs again, so I shift weight, change stride,

try to summon my Zen and ignore it, try
everything except taking the dumb shoe off.
Doffing shoes on a picnic where a cool river
tempts me into testing its smooth stones—fine.

But on the street? Once in shoes and socks
it seems a person is committed. Would I want
people to see me standing one foot in hand
like a numeral four, fumbling with a sock so thin

my pink flesh meshes like a child's face
pressed to a screen? What if the pain is not
in the shoe but in my foot, and now I'm what-ifing
heel spurs, plantar fasciitis, bone cancer,

stumping in a Velcro boot, bumping a walker,
a wheelchair with one leg jacked like a bascule bridge,
or worse—an empty pant leg flopping like
the inflatable weenie man hawking the mattress store.

And now I don't care, so I brace up to a signpost,
rip off the shoe thinking a cracked marble or
bottlecap will clatter out as I braille-read my foot,
strip the sock inside out dreading gym-reek

and then I've got it—the seed of my displeasure,
a small stone smooth as a BB and white
as a milky pearl, and I keep rolling it, just
rolling it between thumb and middle finger.

Warning

How easy it is to shut the damper thinking
the fire is dead. In the morning your sapless mouth
croaks with ash. Or maybe you've done nothing,
and still a skunk bivouacs beneath
the mice-ways and plumbing of your mountain home.
He endows the drapes, a seasonal legacy
creeping out of closets and the sofa's foam.
Ten years ago you told yourself such petty
griefs were nothing but beggar lice, but now
you're finding it harder to shrug and forget the burrs
that seem to stick to everything you know.
It's not the way you want to live, and there's
good reason to keep from keeping that list
you dearly love—those things gone wrong or missed.

The Slipping

Migration is a cumbersome word
for monarch butterflies slipping
through Tunnel Gap. Once he lay
a whole day counting them: a few

orange specks flickered
out of nothing, coasted the hanging
laurel, then dipped away
on Tiffany wings into the blue-

smoked valley. Barely a hundred
in a day he did not mind wasting
then. He had heard old-timers say
that forty years ago the monarchs flew

massed in roiling cloudfire, burning toward
milkweed and the quivering
Mexican forests where they stay
the winter or die. And every fall he must do

the same, as if he, too, heard
some imperious call. He grabs his hiking
boots, camera, and drives the Parkway
to their crossing point. But what is true

slips between the seasons, and
nothing shames him into fleeing
the silent highways
of rutted air and age. And too

many days, like today, he drifts forward
without knowing why, yielding
to each unknowable need, learning his way
as the monarchs straggle through.

Ritual

She stretches, brushing freckled breasts
across his face to set

her rings on the nightstand.
Not a gesture, an amenity—

not to feel
another's gold on his back,

not to hear
any clink in their filigree of logic.

Afterward, a ceremonious silence,
the assumption of vows,
cleaving sanctuary.

Before I Even Get Out of Bed

In the earliest quilted light, as sleep
lifts its own heavy covers, the still,
four-bladed fan uncloaks from the ceiling,
darker swaths against the dark—X.

My spot marked, a rough finger jabs
the treasure map—pirates are coming.
Or maybe it's the signature of an illiterate twin
on papers to have me committed:

he looks up; the doctors nod and point,
and he pens his cross to the page.
Some mornings the fan squares above me
like thick axes on an empty graph

or a plus sign, but what must I add?
And after wine—quadruplet Siamese L's
awaiting deft surgery, freedom to live
in words like *loblolly* and *lullingly.*

But today it's that one
undeflectable image: my name
being x-ed out in the sand,
and someone wishing the tide.

After Deciding to Divorce

Lightning exploded a sweet gum in the Shives' yard
last week, and now on the sidewalk
brown and spiky caricatures, hundreds
of unswept mines.

On my early walk I pass them, thinking about
the lazy news carrier yawning and lofting papers
into the moonless dark, barely catching the curb.
Too-early jonquils flash in a juniper bed—
their brash-as-butter trumpets and emerald stems
brazen yesterday's sleet.

I am here at my far point, cold and dripping
many blocks from home, so who will mind
if I jog across the lawns, pitching rolled papers
toward the morning's steps?

Embracing My Sign at the Chinese Restaurant

Dragon.
Between bites of Kung Pao chicken
I study the placemat menagerie, fold
my tail out of the aisle, huff smoke
through cavernous nostrils.
Eccentric and passionate, I sort
sugar packets from Sweet 'n Lo, know my kiss
stuns like a spoonful of mustard.

Your life is complex.
In an earlier dynasty, I wed another Dragon;
we ended as dueling flamethrowers.
Marry a Monkey or a Rat late in life.
The Monkey I loved was married
and the Rat proved herself, so now I break and open
a fortune: "You will soon create a favorable impression,"
though not on the woman who saw me drop
a tongful of foo yung in the Happy Family.
Her glance skewered me. Again: "You will travel
far and wide, both business and pleasure."

I swing my scaly neck from the booth, rise
over barrows of gold plate, cowed villagers,
torch the odd haystack, my glittering tail
the green sword of morning.

Avoid the Dog.

Planning My Next Incarnation

Drowsing on tossed covers, she idles
through our morning primp, then
trainwrecks into the kitchen,
a shin-buffing breakfast siren.

Daytime she hangs in the window
like spilled pie, watching the slow
circling wind chime. A sleep
contortionist, she stretches out an arc
as hard as a crosscut saw,
but leaps like an outfielder
for thumped paper.

She spirals into laps busy
with book or handwork and sighs
indifferently, glares at every shifting,
her tail an occult and careless wand.

Fantasia Afterthought

    Tottering on a balding hassock,
thick pencil for baton in hand, my son conducts
Dukas and Disney—the Sorcerer's Apprentice.
  His pajama sleeves loose
  as blue pillowcases,
     he steers Mickey toward the wizard's glowing
    moon-starred hat and helps him
        spark a broom to chores.

    But the mouse drowses off, and soon dreams
he is commanding stars and seas, streaking comets,
oceans crashing at his cue. My son flails and rocks
  through this cosmic whimsy,
  embellishing the tale
     with full-mouth *fortes* and heart-jolting leaps
    above the hassock, shrill
        warnings pitched for naught.

    Meanwhile, the broom, hexed with the single-
mindedness of a child, fetches pail after pail
to the overfilled cistern. Swept from dreams to sense,
  Mickey whirlpools toward his
  rashest blunder—raising
     an axe to his helper. The splinters, like small
    lies, come back with their own
        lives: keen, insistent.

    My son conducts hugely, happily
lost in the myth of pure control, oblivious
to those dreams he will prod to life and abandon,

to orders and endings
impossible to charm,
    to gray wizards waiting to dash his work
   to droplets and broom him
        through the splintered air.

Shifting Pictures

I flip open my billfold and credit cards spare keys spill
by the checkout. Squares of papers spiral away—
health insurance, car insurance, renter's, life—
cards for places I am welcomed and punched:
the corner deli, video and coffee shop, anywhere
to buy ten, get the next one free.

The smocked clerk pops gum bubbles while I drop
and scoop the license with old address,
new Visa green and unswiped, push them
back into frayed lining, hazed windows
cracked like a derelict house.

Tonight I shift pictures to a new wallet, stiff
and cow-smelling. Remove the posed three, keep
the brace-tight smile of my son. But he won't fit
in these frosted sleeves. Trim the white border; still no.

Now this again: love him and make him
smaller, choose which arm
to cut from his body.

'A Face To Meet The Faces'

When did photographers first serve "Cheese"
to draw their subject's lips like a theater curtain,
as if the posed had just seen a pratfalling drunk
or a pie plopped in the face of a well-dressed lady?

In the old tintypes, pioneers sit stiff as cornstalks,
their best clothes still shabby, their faces
pinched and blasted as the scrabbled land
indifferent behind the backdrop sheet.

Today heritage is a carnival sepia in a stenciled mat—
a woman floozed out in feather boa and saloon skirt,
her man leathered up in cartridge belts,
Pancho Villa mustache and a dangerous hat.

In the studio the photographer offers me scrims
of unearned lives: a parlor bookcase, apple blossoms
shading a rail fence, a turquoise lagoon
where a palm tree leans in like a lover.

Even basic poses are contortions: knees west, face
east, eyes up, chin down, head cocked
like a happy spaniel. He touches a cord to my nose,
exact distance to my flaws.

Lightning flashes in the silver umbrellas—
posed and poseur, I bare my polished teeth.

Renaissance

Squirrels fussing spirals around an oak
ignore the lowered sky, the jump
of leaf and blade, the heavy
gray smell of rain.

A faint thrumming on the roof,
a pulse deepens in the gutters.
The street goes rabid; curbsides froth
and rush. Hail salts the driveway
with bluish stones, then
relaxes into holographic silver.

The air smokes with changes:
the yellow-gray slant of sharpened sky,
a distant, summer-slow ripping of thunder,
the clear advocacy of jeweled grass.

The English Professor's Flag Football Game

In junior high, so tenuous and spider-limbed
they called him 'Web,' he stepped in front of a pass
one day and, gone! This shocked the roughs, who ran him
shouldered down the field like Stephen Dedalus.
Hurroo! Hurroo! but in truth his laureled ride
was more of a jest to spite the other side.

Once he hooked an eight-iron to within
a foot. Shanked the putt but it rimmed and dropped.
In basketball, a big-lead substitution.
Two years church-league baseball, then he stopped.
Great moments in a non-athletic life.
He watches games on TV with his wife.

So explain this: at forty-one, legs stiff
as student prose, he's playing flag football
with some friends, and with each clumsy shift
and broken run, his agile mind is full
of blood and leather. Something out of temper
has set his aging face like Frank McComber's

and its coppery smell clings, vexing him
to knock the ruddy rector on his ass.
The dentist aches, the lawyer thinks he's lame,
and scornful mouths are baiting, "You want a chance
at glory, Mr. College?" Lecture-steady,
he calls the play he's always dreamed: "Everybody

go long, and I will get it there." He takes
the snap, whirls and looks but no one's free,
and now he's sprinting like an egg on toothpicks,
running, running for his life is Mercury,

Atalanta, swift Camilla, for his life is flying,
speeding, skimming along the main with wings
the closing rout have almost trimmed,
but today, oh yes, today! They will not catch him!

Swing Away

I'm the first adult at the piñata so I wrap hands
to the taped-up Slugger as someone ties a jersey
over my eyes, spins me three or four times
though it's been only minutes since I fielded
two beers and an underdone burger while kids
whapped at the rainbow donkey but couldn't crack it,
its multi-hued hide ribboning into thin pennants.

Jeers and heckles ratchet up as pogoing kids beg me to
split the seams of that parti-pony so they can
dive for Dum-Dums, Slo-Pokes, Skittles and Smarties,
grab Cow Tales, Dubble Bubble and Tootsie Roll Midgees,
    but I keep
missing it, whip nothing but air off dizzy blind-ump stumbles,
    and each
whiff rockets laughter so I know something's up and a peek
catches my neighbor yanking the rope, one jackass jerking another,
and I'd like to step over and bust his burro-brain with a Ruthian rip
just to see what peanuts spill from that crackerjack crown

but it's his batboy's party, stubby grounder I once saw muscle
    my own tyke's
tricycle away and run it into the street. *Let him hit it, for*
    God's sake!
the mothers scream, and all annoyance melts away; my body calms
as I plant my right foot, shift weight back and turn
the hips, pull shoulders high to cock that bat like I am
swinging for legend status—61, 715—first candy blasted
into low earth orbit, sweet missiles clearing fences as they rise.

Gong Show

Squirrels are crashing cymbals on my propane tank,
every careless walnut a seismic skip
in the measured soundtrack of my street:
geese clarinets, piccolo phoebes, the sad
cello of doves. Each percussive whang
bangs my thoughts like a knocked colander
and another slick idea wriggles down the disposal.

I'd like to pop those squirrels with a slingshot
but my aim is bad, and each miss would
power a piece of pea gravel onto the green
metal roof of my third-neighbor-over. Maybe I'll
pump my Daisy with five strong squeezes and bark them
off the branch like old hunters did, a concussive kill
sparing fur for gloves and flesh for stew. But I don't

want to gut and skin squirrels; I want them to stop
dropping gongs while I'm trying to write. I don't care
if the Grand Vizier announces a husband for the princess.
I don't care what celebrity judges think of my act.
I'm not conducting "Overture" from *Tommy* here,
I just want those rodents to fall out and scratch
some forgettable holes, bury the fallen.

Cartoons dress them cute but squirrels are only
one winter clothes promotion above mice: sweatered
Cossack rats squat dancing across the yard squalling "Hey!"
At the movies I watch them zip as goggled sidekicks
and antic schemers but never see them swinging upside
down from a bird feeder raking in seed with
two claws while I shovel a bucket of popcorn.

Rural Icon

In Grant Wood's *American Gothic,*
the gripped pitchfork's stiff verticality
imposes: cut of the farmer's coat,
board and batten siding, the bosomless woman's
bird neck. And what curves is comfortless:
his spectacles hard as dollars, the cameo clasped
at her throat, an untucked tendril of hair.
She is used to looking away, closing herself
like the curtained rooms, brown shades
dull as her shapeless dress.

Very little risks the level plane: the porch's
roofline, flat as a tight smile, divides the lower panes
from the upper's arched bullets. Even his heart
falls on the plumb, chest seams of his overalls
ghosting the steel-tined fork.

The Jigsaw Puzzle from the Second-Home Thrift Store

is missing seven pieces, now that we can count
the unaccounted for, amorphous cousins absent
from this family mottle. Their truancy reveals
brown amoeba voids in our panorama of cowboys
chasing mustangs, a beautiful Palomino shattering
sage and cactus as it flames around chuckholes

dark as the dining room table, little misshapen caves
of knobs and sockets, a Freudian mosaic with
discrete omissions, none touching, none
betraying the gray underside of desire.
Still, we miss the cousins who cannot see
the space we built for this reunion, how we

laid out a level floor, squared up corners and
framed the sides, then carefully raftered clouds
into a turquoise sky. They leave ghost shapes hovering
in the high plains air, a blazing horse stretched
beyond the uncoiled lariat.

III

A Lesson on the Immaterial

At the corner of North and Main, a street preacher
paces like the cougar in our city zoo.
He hounds the Saturday shoppers who grudge him room
as he scribbles the morning with a bony finger,
punctuating scripture with jabs and shouts.
He exhorts women leaving the lingerie shop,
raves at men who wheel away and smoke.

For as long as I can remember, some cheerless scholar
from the local seminary has worked this corner.
One Saturday years ago, a braid of boys surged
from the dingy, downtown theater and slammed
a pimpled preacher. His eyes drew down to bullets
as he said "The earth will swallow you up
and your bodies burn in everlasting fire!"
We hung mid-breath, afraid to cough until
he turned to resume his rant and our knot untied itself,
fraying wildly toward our waiting homes.

I cannot say whether heat or memory
goads me now to ask him if this works, has he
ever saved anyone? But I am shocked to see
he is old, someone's father, no student proselytizer,
and caged behind his anger he waits for me to speak
but looks through me as if I am but air.

Sign People

All torso and angled appendage,
their disc heads float
on thin rims of collar:

black-and-yellow dwellers of the school zone,
faceless loiterers at crosswalks, steep-trail heralds
with a block of backpack, bathroom monitors
in bell-skirts and blunt limbs, or
a genderless blend.

How unlike us, these shadows
of caution and propriety, presuming to lead
without feet, hands, eyes.

What the Famous Writer Said

'Do not confuse a shoe with juicy steak'
seems reasonable but rather unneeded advice.
I can't imagine liking at any price
a loafer on the grill, an odd mistake
I'd need be passing drunk or daft to make.
Maybe a sly reversal—a pair of iced
ribeyes used as sandals might suffice
for a bloody day, but there'd be dogs to shake.

So what's it all about? A metaphor
of self-delusion, haste, or treadless schemes?
After weeks at sea Columbus' crew
thought the difference less profound; their hunger
effaced all lines that sense and compass knew.
Sometimes, all you have to eat are dreams.

Friends in Denali

Snow plumes from the summit like a crisp pennant.
They wake to silver air and a peak
in rose linen shaping itself with light,

the same light that drags burn from shadow
on my deck six time zones away.
I could be wrong—

their day wet and whipping, the mountain
packed in an angry locker of clouds.
When they call I will know,

but like so many truths it will not matter
what the light dreamed there,
what the shadow kept here.

After the Doctor Said No

The detector shrills me out of bed.
I shove my wife, lurch into stinging smoke,
then we stumble down the hall to save the children.
But they think this early rousting is a game
and run away slamming doors, hiding
their blurred faces behind storybooks
and dragging familiar toys, criss-
crossing the hall in cartoon chase
while rafters snap like small bones.
We slog through smoke, screaming
as it rides us down like dark water.

Later, on the lawn, we cannot speak.
Yellow rainsuits pick for scorched books
and blankets; their vague, grimed faces
will not look at us in borrowed sheets.
A man stops, bends down, and says
'Over here,' and as we circle he lifts
a blackened timber with his boot

and I wake up, startled, in the quiet house.
All I hear is my wife's even breathing.
I walk down the hall opening doors,
but I see the same silent furniture
and toyless floors
where no crib will ever rest.

Right Now in the Attic Crawl Space

Something is moving above the sheetrock
ceiling of my apartment. Its steps
are too heavy for squirrel

or rat. Above the window
behind the barrister, where the eave
narrows to a wedge of heat and light

rising through the soffit,
the intruder circles and settles
its stiff fur against drywall.

I wait, then rap the ceiling
with a broom, and something pads away
across the dining room.

It is back in minutes. Standing
in a chair, I hear squeaks and chittering.
Whatever it is, it has given birth.

How is it I never heard
this feral mother, raccoon or possum,
scraping the insulation into a nest?

I did not hear her
numberless trips fetching leaves
and green sticks that would keep

the pink fiberglass from salting
the raw skin of her kits.
On either side of the pebbled ceiling

we both are listening now.

Midnight Crossing

From the steps of the cottage slanting
back from the sand, we watch
orange lightning spark the horizon,

strobe clouds in midnight crossing,
ancient barges fluent in gold, purple
sails spreading for the run.

Miles away, that ocean storm
dazzles with keen phrasing,
enough power to quicken the sea.

Here beside you, my brightest words
flare and scatter over silent dunes,
the muted surf.

Diminuendo

Letter
Words slip under my shirt,
a script of kisses.
I unpage your laces
and dream you
sheer as paper.

Call
Our voices
tightwire the distance,
balancing
between promise and
propriety.

Visit
Having abstracted the weather
and recited our family précis,
we sit and
stare at our
crumpled hands.

Counting My Daughter's Boyfriends on One Hand

Thumb

Rhymes with dumb. Opposable
in every way. Plenty of grip
but no grasp. Popular with babies,
vending machines and hammers.
Extend yourself, bud; move on.

Index

This kid's on point, can trace it out:
valedictorian, Bachelor's, Duke Med then
City General, silver BMW and a lake house.
Boasts a letter sweater and a trophy shelf.
Boy is cock-sure. Pun intended.

Middle

Who gets the digital salute?
The one who honks from the street, then oils
to the door in a Busch t-shirt. "Nice,"
he says, scanning her like an MRI.
"Better stay that way," I say, patting my holster.

Ring

Seems promising. Know his family from church.
Brings flowers, says "Mr." and "Mrs."
Opens doors and offers to mow.
Can make and take a joke. Daughter says
"He's so nice. And boring."

Little

Runt sausage, slender twig. She hates
I call him Pinky. Artistic, athletic enough
for chess. Shouts Jeopardy! answers.
"So smart," she says. Brain power
can't raise him off the sofa, though, or lift grocery sacks.

Lined up, side-by-side, they make
a good slap.

Kitchen Inventory

Measuring Cups

Placed on the counter to dry,
they line up like a Catholic family photo,
siblings in regular gradations,
from big brother's full cup
to baby sister's eighth.

They fill to serve, clear
and precise, keeping matters
in proportion, never
going to excess, always
having a handle on things.

Grater

Knuckle-rougher, fierce
exfoliator, will knock the zest
off any lemon.
No cleft of knife, but
a hundred scallops.
What we can't have in full
we'll take by the shreds.

Turkey Baster

Made to rain liquor
over roasting fowl
but also useful as
gasoline siphon,
rattlesnake-bite suction bulb,
otoscope for a bear
or cow tracheotomy.

Wire Whisk

A silver tornado between the hands.
Hummingbird cage, fairy prison.
Airy provocateur who stirs things up.
Warning to all ingredients:
You will be assimilated.

Wine Opener

Palm derrick, twisting
its bit into a sunken plug
as side scaffolds rise
like silver arms of a priestess
here to bless this pull, pop
and fruition.

Now breathe.

Goldfish with Issues

Mine is a small
round duty, a patrol
tight as lighthouse
stairs, routing neons
hourly from this plastic
castle. They think
their quick transparency
hides them, but I
see their true colors—
electric jazz and
flash, that's all—
garish as the rainbow gravel.

And what reward?
I am barely remembered—
an occasional shake
from the can while
the walkers fin the shelves
for that small paddle
of buttons they aim
while eating from
hinged boxes or papers
bright as a Yellow Tang.

When they settle,
less mouthing occurs.
Pat as a pair
of bivalve wings,
they stare into
the flat tank of flux
and color, blink
now and then,
but no bubbles.

In Concert

In an open-air auditorium I'm drifting,
appeased by violins and flutes,
when I glimpse a black moth looping

the white shafts of spotlights, slow-spiraling
down, keeping its course with a circuit
of minute tiltings. It is nothing

but motion against stillness, and I
am about to let it go its artless way
when for several timeless measures

the moth whirls twinned to the swelling music:
pirouetting with the strings, gliding
easily over the reeds, a quick turn

timed to a flourish of tympani.
It was a ballet as brief as a dream.
Later, my friends say "pure coincidence,"

but that raven-moth now prompts me
to see things unscripted and unscored,
such casual gifts winging the mutable air.

Resolve

Think of all the things that will
never be accomplished: avoiding
robocalls, understanding
God, concocting a riskless pill

that piques happiness. Even
sorting the bundled years of vacation
snapshots or the slides stacked in yellow
boxes, unlabeled, unculled, seems no

more likely than remembering
the birthdays and children of cousins.
Yet this is why we dress and go
to hear the grand symphony—

adagio to *allegro vivace,*
to see the tragedy in five acts
and a curtain call, to laugh at the story-
teller while he loops the slack

rope of belief around our necks
and nooses it. All things resolve
in an auditorium, but what of
lost jackets, unanswered letters,

smiles that dry into civility, or worse?
So we paint a bathroom mauve,
savor crème brûlée on heirloom dishes,
whisper ten minutes of pianissimo kisses.

The Moon's Face Opens in Song

Stars are dragging webbed chairs
toward the campfire of her voice.
Clustered under quilts, they tip
plaid thermoses as marshmallows
flame and fall, then belt out camp songs
louder every round until
they quaver near to collapse.

One spry star, around since the beginning,
uncorks a jug of shine and pours some
into a leaky dipper. "Have you heard," he asks,
"why the moon never shows her backside?"

"Do *not* tell that story," the moon cautions,
but the old star winks, takes a long
draw from the jug. "Was this
young comet came through here once,"
he drolls, and settles back to tell.

Day Tour

Geese fly over, honking their klaxons
like a caravan of Model T's, then drop and rally
in the neighbor's pond, raucous and flapping.

A few step out on the weedy bank
to browse and haggle like it's market day
at every pond and field and stubble-yard,

but most circle like a motor club cruising
a town square, proud owners in black
chauffeur's caps and white scarves.

Soon all lift into a skein of order and gabble,
wheeling a smooth county circuit
over old roads mapped in their heads.

The Pull

In a hospital room my young son
watches me watch my father.
I smooth the white hair, spoon

applesauce and coax down
granulated pills. For an hour
my son is still and sound-

less as a prayer. He stares
at the bed, looking for
the old man in the overstuffed chair

who reads to him about buffalo.
The respirator whispers a soft
language we almost think we know,

telling us—what? That we are
past the embarrassment of legs
thin and purple as weedstems, a catheter

that falls off, brown phlegm
that rises like a tide? My son
is restless now and ready. For him

the hours seem to pull everything
along, nothing stays. He turns
from the mirror and tugs my arm, singing

"Da-ad." And in that fluted syllable
I hear my life breaking
into bits of *have, had*, and *will*.

I touch what I am given
and what I must give up,
and even if I were to summon

a strength as resistless
as the striding minutes, I could
never pull from me all my selfishness.

Father and son, each frail
with years, drift beyond
all love, all will.

'Oh! Blessed Rage For Order'

I never saw my father shop for anything
except grass seed and groceries, maybe
a wrench or a box of nails. Still,

in the middle of washing a load of socks,
my mother would answer the door
and there would be a workman

with a washing machine strapped to a dolly.
She had learned not to say "There must be
some mistake," for there was never any mistake,

only socks dripping like clumps of wet bark
in a hastily-cleared sink. At supper
she would say into her peas, "The washer

was fine, dear." But he had heard
something in the grind of its gears
and bearings that argued past her.

He was the same with dying.
I always thought he'd pass away while sleeping,
but he could not sue the time, and it troubled him.

Still, a month was all he spent on dying.
Time for whispered conversations with his wife,
friends' visits, blessings to his sons.

"No machines," he said, and later,
"No more food." We sat with him and waited.
He died with the preacher in the room.

We found a note in his tidy bureau
addressed to her. What to do
with all the bank accounts, how to

divest the stocks, when the car should go
for service, the kind of seed and lime
to buy for spring.

Before the Fog Burns Off

What is the good of gray?
Death pallor, dullness, the hue of dust,
ashes and old age, nothingness.
Gray lacks commitment and carries rain.
Gray hums, neither song nor whistle,
the very color of ambivalence.

What is the good of gray?
An elm's shadow in a snowfield,
rainwebs and worn silver.
Gray mediates and soothes the eye.
Gray robes the mountain valleys,
the flannel sage of morning.

Please Stand

Praise to the people who read directions
before assembling the bookcase, and praise to the people
who don't and say, "Where does this piece go?"
Huzzah to lovers of multi-lane freeway, its interposing grass
and routine facilities, and hip-hip to drivers happy when
roadwork shunts them onto a shoulderless byway.

We salute all ritual beginnings—green flags
and baptisms, the elegant unfolding of napkins.
We salute the impulse too—ordering the novel entrée
or taking an uncleared trail. Hallowed are
all humble acts of courage: hands
trembling over a keyboard, waving a child
off to school, unpacking a suitcase
that has just been packed.

We honor the private ceremonies of continuance, when
just getting dressed is a prayer. Honor upon all uncheered miles
pedaled or run in rain. Honor to those who show up,
who keep promises made in public, keep the ones
silent and heavy as snow.

Praise for the rich soil of hope, for the precious seeds,
and for hands working, many hands, more than enough.

Absolute Faith

What was it I was thinking about, driving
home that night, turning over some unmade
choice like a set of keys in a coat pocket
when a fox leapt from a laurel brake
just as my headlights swept the curve.
Exposed, spotlighted in mid-arc, he twisted
back upon himself as lithe and fluid
as a whip, so that his rear paws touched instead
of the front, and he was back in the woods he leapt from.

I think it the most graceful movement
I have ever seen, pure suppleness, like a wreath
of red smoke touching a breeze. Such a moment
terrifies, such ease in changing direction,
without plans, wholly committed to a move
and then undoing it, without caprice,
just absolute faith in opposites, seconds apart.

If Not These Things

Peering into a mountain cabin
you salute the window like a scout,
spying trout cushions and carved bar stools.
Safe on this vacant deck, the two of you
spoon in a chaise, gazing down
at a windless denim lake.

After dark you drift the campground loops
while small fires whisper and wink.
Stars have sugared the sky
and you could pour your voices
into a crystal flute and drink.

You pass the tent for now,
touchstepping the dark
to an empty site and table.
Nothing has ever seemed so close,
not the bright city of stars
nor the black intaglio of trees,
not legs wreathed with yours
nor a face warm in your palms,

and if not these things then what
is one day in all
your life?

New Song

Asphalt shimmers, curves to woods that lean
and whisper on days I don't block everything
with a helmet of rock and roll, somebody like The Doors
rescinding the petty orders of the day,
slamming the mopish *yes* and querulous *no*
into a cave that's black and deep and crystalline.

Susie trots with me, up the grade and back,
into the woods and out, no thought to impress
with her two miles to every one of mine.
The road's edge is her world: wet, black leaves
and a sorority of smells, ears cocked like a pair of sevens,
ready to charge the laurel on a squirrel's dare
or to sack the green village of sparrows.

I'm pushing palm against thigh when Susie
takes off over the hill right as Ray Manzarek
takes off on the organ interlude of "Light My Fire."
He works and reworks the same plane of notes,
stairsteps down then back up before teasing
into Krieger's lyrical, Eastern guitar.

It's the way love pulls you toward a silver wall,
lifts you, lifts you to a bright, airless zone
where you will gladly trade breath
for one more tenuous moment.

When I meet my dog on the downslope
she is writhing in the weeds by the runoff ditch,
legs pedaling, growling the low guttural of joy.

She whips upright, shakes pointlessly
as I speak but I can't hear my voice
above the new song rising in my ears.
She noses my hand, then lopes up the road
whirling and snapping at bees.

About the Author

Kenneth Chamlee is Emeritus Professor of English at Brevard College in North Carolina. His poems have appeared in *The North Carolina Literary Review, Cold Mountain Review, Worcester Review, Naugatuck River Review, Weber: The Contemporary West,* and many others, including several editions of *Kakalak: An Anthology of Carolina Poets.* He has published two award-winning chapbooks, *Absolute Faith* (ByLine Press) and *Logic of the Lost* (Longleaf Press). Ken holds a Ph.D. in English/Creative Writing from UNC-Greensboro and was the first director of the Looking Glass Rock Writers' Conference (Brevard, NC). He teaches in the Great Smokies Writing Program of UNC-Asheville and has served as a Gilbert-Chappell Distinguished Poet with the North Carolina Poetry Society.

Ken enjoys visiting waterfalls and listening for owls when camping in the mountains of western North Carolina. He has lifelong interests in outdoor photography and landscape art and has written a poetic biography of painter Albert Bierstadt, *The Best Material for the Artist in the World* (Stephen F. Austin University Press). Learn more at www.kennethchamlee.com.

Printed in the USA
CPSIA information can be obtained
at www.ICGtesting.com
LVHW041824191023
761576LV00002B/282